www.finishinglinepress.com

[neurotic love baby]

poems by

Marie Conlan

Finishing Line Press
Georgetown, Kentucky

[neurotic love baby]

ACKNOWLEDGMENTS

Thank you to Metatron Press for selecting this manuscript as a finalist for
the Metatron Rising Author's Award in 2018, and featuring a brief selection
of poems on their website and Instagram.

Thank you to *Pidgeonholes* magazine for publishing "Dreams & Grief & Love
Things," a poem derived from various lines of this book.

Thank you to Yesica Mirambeaux for this gorgeous cover.

Infinite gratitude to TJ, for everything. To Gabrielle Joy Lessans, Heather
Sweeney, Jenni Ashby, Shawnie Hamer, Jake Grieco, and Sara Veglahn for
their eyes and insight on this book in its various forms. Gabby, thank you
for fueling the energy & magic & discipline to get it done—writing would
be lonely without you. To all the minds & hearts of JKS and the 2016 & 2017
Naropa Summer Writing Program, thank you, thank you, thank you.

Publisher: Leah Huete de Maines
Editor: Christen Kincaid
Cover Art and Design: Yesica Mirambeaux
Author Photo: Marie Conlan

Order online: www.finishinglinepress.com
also available on amazon.com

Author inquiries and mail orders:
Finishing Line Press
P. O. Box 1626
Georgetown, Kentucky 40324
U. S. A.

Table of Contents

[home making]

How do you feel about ferns? I would like them in all of my entryways. I would like a pocket for all of my stones. Isn't it silly I keep trying to tell you. Dirt mixes with blood, dust with sweat. Clump the body back together. So, you read my legs. Do you feel guilty or do I. Do you remember if you said my thighs were fields of Saturdays, or peonies [?] I remember, they are the shape of sevens. You gripped them by the handles.

A man at the hardware store tells us which flowers will grow and which will not. We want beer & poppies & red buckets. We want them in plenty to stack around our throats, crowns, bathrooms. Sometimes we vomit in the middle of gardening, or building, or sleeping.

In the spring we pluck the heads of roses. We roll them between our palms into balls of tight, leaking petals. We offer them to each other as offerings. Here: could be anything. Could hold any sentiment. Free memories.

In the winter we push dead aspen trees onto the ground to hear the cold crack of the roots. To feel our hands. We carry the dead limbs and stack them into a pile. They are to become made things. Fences for keeping in & out.

How many things do you own? Thousands. If you count the corona bottles and the fake fireplace logs. Infinity, more. The cap of an acorn is good for holding blue things. Stones or sea water. I could write into my eyelids, and that could be enough writing for a long time, if I chose the right words and blended them into the phosphene with tedious precision. I tried to write. The best lovers are pinching at their knuckles, examining the sensation of bleeding. Pinching a little too hard.

Yes, I want my hair pulled into a bow. Launch me into the snow puddles. Tie a ribbon around me and brace for either a containing or a breaking, you may choose any color. The thinner the ribbon the more you will be unable to distinguish me from it.

goodmorning baby, I've written you a poem. In the poem you are a

sepia rinse & I keep seeing your face bloom from the inside of my

mouth, but I am telling you my mouth does not open, the whole

time it does not open. I rub your knuckles into hills.

I like the part where you turn red with sudden shyness.

Lets grow old in a tourist town. Remember how you didn't think

you'd grow old [?]

errands: blue lighter,
mescaline, accident, bat
guano, tomato babies, stale
licorice, three pastel sunset,
your favorite part, fresh
pyrex, dahlias soaked in
ash.

Four inches of snow in May. We cannot afford groceries. We go

into the store to pee & we leave with a cherry pie and two fishing

licenses. Next week, we watch an old man steal a caramel from the

candy bins and chew it while his wife pays for roasted chicken.

Every time you rub the line of my spine you tenderize me into a

pulp I am waiting for you to discard at the bottom of your morning

juice.

*   *   *   *   *   *   *   *   *

  *   *   *   *   *   *   *   *

*   *   *   *   *   *   *   *   *

  *   *   *   *   *   *   *   *

*   *   *   *   *   *   *   *   *

If it were me, I would still dream about you coming dressed in red & placing poppies on my cheeks. You might shake cinnamon into my jean pockets, pour milk, come in chewing tourmaline & repeating colors to me. Your blood turned to picnic tables easily. Then turned to soil, dropped palmfuls into my mouth & you packed it with bat guano. I grew peppers. We made stew. Heat from oven, light from refrigerator. All of today's needs from kitchen organs.

Something about the beetle kill reminds me of the face you'd make while scrambling eggs. Anticipatory happiness. Reminds me of your outstretched palm. Blooming a fist of wilting taco bell.

We hold very still and let our time & space fabric baby catch up. I push the aloe over, I push the gravel to the other side of the driveway, I strike your small hair. We have never caught up, we have never caught up.   My blood moves from left artery to kitchen flood, my nails grow from cuticle to ripped crescents, your hand to my ankle & we have never caught up. We have never caught up.

When I hold your grief it sews a red thread into mine.

Knuckles are hills, if you want to salvage this.

Crawl up & try to find eyes.

Every choice is so big.

& you you you you

[neurotic love baby]

Thumbs like torn paintings. Eyes like ponds stretched over the plains of the middle west. I keep drinking from this earth & ending up in your eyes. I keep clawing at this earth like I am unscrewing your spine from you your fucking spine all broken I climb your vertebrae like stones I throw them like stones away from you get that body off of you it hurts it hurts I almost lost you to the government I almost lost you to paroxetine I almost lost you to Chicago I almost lost you to the highway I almost lost you to a dream & where's your god damn bones now pull the boot straps

we'll run

we'll run

we'll run

I want to leave you for a life I don't know. I want to leave you for under the bed when you get so fucking mad about air conditioners & car rotors & I could find a corner of carpet to crawl under. Wait until you notice a shifting lump in the room before I unfold from my dippy child shapes. I want to leave you for a world that is nicer to you & we can meet up at the magnolias. I want to leave when the mornings become a slaughterhouse. I'd rather watch people I am indifferent to turn themselves to pulp. I have questions: What if the deer get to the garden. What if the dog dies. What if we forget how to put a Sunday together and the aspen trees make for bad burial grounds & I forget the words to my name. I am just saying. What if I die and turn to ghost waiting for you & I miss it & I am trapped here all alone what if they don't tell me how to get to god & I am left wandering the realms like Chicago like how I was wandering Chicago all without you. We can do this afraid. What if a leaving.

If I were going to write myself all over you what font could I use for the elbows? How many breaths should I lend? How many colors should I mix into the eyelids? If the backdrop is the pink glow of a salt lamp. Is the skyline of cheek. Do I rub the stained sunshine from the gums? Do I bother with the organs?

Wouldn't you look tragic. In a Nebraska cornfield all red &
windblown & wheat-haired, a bloodroot tucked neatly
behind your ear, wilting, sun-drunk, crumbling down your
eyelashes. As a child you would lick everything you were
curious about. Car tires & lightbulbs & dead wasps. Your
father said don't be weird, so now you don't. But your tongue.
Still appears earth-strung. When it reaches my collarbone, it
recognizes the rich flavor of a wound.

Part of our love story is stuck onto the underside of the Mendota Bridge, where I pushed my entire fist down my throat for a memory wedged deep between bones. Blue green & pulsing. Blue green like cold jade sweating from hot breath, rich & hearty & wet with life. We peeled it from inside of me with quick, deliberate fingers while we were walking and you were sweatshirt wrapped & moon faced. We slapped it against the concrete spine of the bridge, gummy & glistening. My baby cadger. Ready to harden in the shade of a city & hatch into our new thing, right down the Mississippi River. Float straight shot to Texas and grow big. Slide into the ocean sunburned & shaking & spreading its face to the ocean as an offering, its dying words "Big." So big, bigger than a body.

your ankles dipped into the red barn. your legs a sparrow, a quiet frenzy in the ancient breeze. hello your goodbye swallow & swollen lung against the wet grain—

The pillow case a shriveled stench of bacon grease. Hair tied in blueberry knots. You kept a bruise under your middle fingernail for a whole three days after coming home. In this memory, I have stitched the lining with lace, I have painted the lace a softening blue, I have tamed the little pink nostalgia, I have painted it on the walls, I have tucked old hands in soil and watered wormhole mouths with milk. When you grow new ends, please wrap us in tender curtains. Please preserve something.

Sometimes I am sending you an embrace from your dead friend in a dream & when I wake up I know you have had this dream too. You never remember the embrace. Sometimes I am taking you to the doctor's office. Where does the blood come from? The dream. I awake inside my hand. I am very blue, and tucked neatly behind the smooth valleys of my knuckles.

Bucolic knees. The edges of your eyes go all field against ocean. Petrichor breath. Tornado in your jacket sleeve. Smell of frying potatoes & earthworm casting. Of a lingering cedar that has stained your neck & never rinsed. Last minute savior. A fern stretched across scar tissue.

I am ready to crumble into seed & be swept into an open watering.

We find a motel 6 on the edge of an old cowboy town still dressed in gold mines and saloon doors. When I step out of the car I shrink down and down and down until I am the size of a baby doll sewn with sand, belly filled with red highway poppies.

I cannot give my drawings heads. I almost lost you. I   a white room,

darling.

Way down me go. Hands clasped around so tightly. Press harder. Make space between my skin and your skin. Press with a heat that is welding. Harder. Sever the new oneness & repeat again again again & again. I want to know my separateness while I can. Know the one do you understand. Do I explain myself well. Press harder. Again & again & again.

[I   a   white room]

You say: I know a thing or two about bird law. You say: you

see? How the wings are beginning to glow? How she nose-

dives towards the surface? She is ready so so much to

become a newthing, dust or animal.

While I am listening, I am thinking. Stick me with pine needles. I would

like to dress like outside. And beginning.

Instructions for afternoon:
Face me. Loop a bloodroot
neatly around my ring finger.
Wait for it to crumble
onto my ankles. Keep me still.
Lace a rope through my ribcage
and anchor me.
Soften the soil, if necessary.
I could take root.
Someday I could be
for keeps for real.

Let me hold your knees
against each other.
My life lines
flood with sweat.
Little rivers pooling
in your desert hills.

Little panic baby give me
your bellybutton
a snow globe
your dust shaking
down elbows give me
something fragile
to fit in my palms.

You paint my corners a soft pink & crouch down into the color

you have given me. In the morning you pick another color.   I

a   white room.

        I don't know how to say it shaped me that as a child you

        tried to   shoot   you   realize how

        big   you

bullet jammed   almost lost   you & before

    I climb into that and   [?] You said defeated but

    did you think it funny at   all how

    big   you

[the ending]

I thought he sang:

share my

mood

I thought he sang:

at   least

I   know

alive,

&   still—

Tell me a story. What am I but what I am always trying to get you to do to me. What is it about spelling the shape of you with my throat that makes me so unable to distinguish my reflection. What does it mean to have pushed my palm into yours. You be the small desert, I'll be the city sewage tunnel. Climb through me to the mountains. Happily ever after. Spell me into a snowstorm. I tattooed your thigh with a rose next to other roses that were not mine. Spelled you into infinity. I remind you this one is mine. Happily ever after.

If you were to try

you would appear so

below you might

use names might

use two different

     might need

practice.

A dark there

facing down

a dark corresponding

facing

a double whole.

Look at this time.

Everything cut in half.

Even the where

should be. Halved.

in this brief bed I spill labyrinths on your stomach from sugar packets. I tuck the pink wrapper behind your ear, I cannot find my way out I leave pine needles in all of the corners I have been.

to eat the crumbles to paste to
wake the sleeping to sleep against
the sleeping to be late and
necessary to hold your keys out
and demand an opening to fit
better when poured with water to
push out to exit to expand inside
of the exit to believe in the ability
for arms to rise and over the head
and keep and forget your
telephone on the carpet to be
deliberate to know the best feeling
in the world and forget how to go
there to know the way and forget
any way to go

```
*       *       *       *       *       *       *       *       *
    *       *       *       *       *       *       *       *
*       *       *       *       *       *       *       *       *
    *       *       *       *       *       *       *       *
*       *       *       *       *       *       *       *       *
```

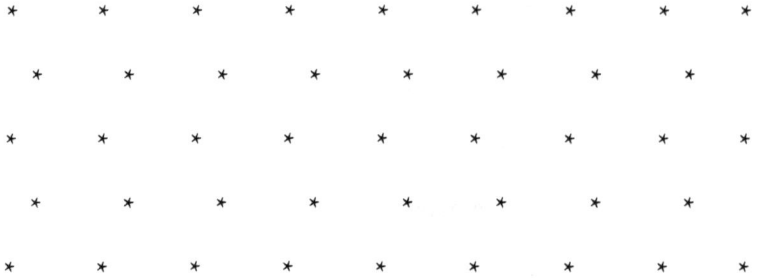

Do you want to know where I separate [?]

[and still]

I am scared of heights so you build me a railing. I am splitting into unequal halves. You hold my cheeks like apples, pushing them gently against the core. I feel like a bad comedown & your arms could be anything: a part of a body, a stone, a chevy engine, mine.

I'll throw them in the goddamn river next time you mention   I
swear to god I will   should have   you please don't   and me please
do not do not ever I swear to god—

I've swallowed you whole. I had a hard time fitting your knee through the space between my molars. The sheet of cut up cheek stretched wide wide into an O. You did not fit. Sometimes my breath carries residue of your muted exhales, sometimes wrinkles into laughter. It took my home of a body to get that much sound out of you. I mean me. It took two bodies to get that much sound out of me.

I want to give you everything. Here: a warm plate. Here: the juicy snot from our cacti's fresh flesh wound. Here: an action shot of Barbie's pussy, an action shot of my pussy, a glock wiped clean, a colic child, a wilting stain. Will you take these from me? I mean, as a gift. I mean, as a drug. I left a piece of tobacco in the belly of a hot red poppy for you, it was bulging with grief. Here: a dream.

I have questions for you. Is the inside of your cheek bruised from the violent sucking of dandelions, or the soft erosion of your own tongue? I'll be eastern California and you be a Nevada sewer. I'll climb through you like I could ever get under you. Like I could ever feel the small wall of some blazing labyrinth. What if the grapefruit sticks to our throats and we ferment into silence? And if we pretend not to notice? What if and. We leave a day behind & mourn it years later. We swallow its dust every night & heave it into the drawers of our nightstands each morning. We wonder how the wind rattles our organs into memory. You remind me of a memory I haven't had before. Some quivering.

Did you mean it like this [?] If my body is northeast Minneapolis and your tongue gets stuck in a peak 9 avalanche, how fast does the freeway end. Doesn't a flower feel like a spectacle to you & doesn't a dug up carrot feel like a broken limb of the earth. Do you want to know how the valley of my hip tastes. Fluorescent. Yes yes yes. Tell me a story. What am I always trying to get you to do to me.

Spell me wrong. Paint the pink onto my ribs. The ribs are lava! The ribs are lava! You jump between them eloquently, but you blister nonetheless. You seem to be in my tradition. I revived at least a neck from the drawing, but it is sliced like lunch meat. Cotton socks for everyone in the kingdom. No more allergies, and fingers that don't soak the stench of salt.

Would you pick the song for dying. Rip the stitched flowers from the curtains and press them against your piano. Play dahlia, play the yellow daisy, play worm casting, play back surgery, play leave, play wake up, play your crescent bruise, play doorway—

Up north we carry a belief in ourselves. We hold hands over the center counsel & think of rolling out from the car. Still attached to each others hands. Watch the metal contort from collision & curl into the rock outcropping a mile out from the highway, build a night from pebbles & sleep on whatever fallen patch of sunset. Go back for the headlights and coddle them like the moon, eat them for light, sweet & lo dreams, the sharp crunch of glass. Our bloodied mouths filled with moon, our hands with hands with hands with moon with blood.

I am throwing cold rocks at doors. I am speaking to my beloved now. The sun rains. The horizon looks magnificently like your eye. The snow line is your cheek and you push push the clouds into you, curl into the corner of a sky wound and shake like lightning all night. Little light junkie.

Cannot get closer than push push into you. Delirious with fear. Starting to lose you. Call me at the end of the flat irons. When you can pull off into dirt road and tell me: the way there is nothing and then something so high. And tell me: the ground is magnificent against the birth of a mountain. Tell me again: how it is the pushed edge of a wound, and you are standing inside of its rupture.

*   *   *   *   *   *   *   *   *
   *   *   *   *   *   *   *   *
*   *   *   *   *   *   *   *   *
   *   *   *   *   *   *   *   *
*   *   *   *   *   *   *   *   *

Marie Conlan is an artist living and writing in Colorado. She received her MFA from the Jack Kerouac School of Disembodied Poetics at Naropa University. She was named a finalist for the Noemi Press Book Award for Prose in 2017 and 2018, a finalist for the Airlie Press Prize in 2018, and a finalist for Metatron's 2018 Rising Author's Prize. Her first book *Say Mother Say Hand: an anti-memoir* was published by Half Mystic Press.

www.ingramcontent.com/pod-product-compliance
Lightning Source LLC
Chambersburg PA
CBHW021203090426

42740CB00008B/1207